Judy Garland

Little Woman, Big Talent

by John Briggs

D1511083

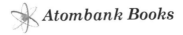 *Atombank Books*

Published by Atombank Books, Guilderland, NY

Edited by Albany Editing, Scotia, NY

Cover Photo: CBS promotional photo, 1956

Back Cover Photo: Audio-animatronic characters from *The Wizard of Oz* at Walt Disney World's Hollywood Studio

Biography: Judy Garland: Little Woman, Big Talent by John Briggs. The life of actress and singer Judy Garland (1922-1969). Hollywood's Golden Age.

ISBN: 978-0-9905160-2-6

To Johnny K and Hailey Boo (my own little dancer)

TABLE OF CONTENTS

LITTLE GIRL, BIG TALENT

Long before Judy Garland was famous for playing Dorothy in *The Wizard of Oz*, she was a little girl growing up in the tiny town of Grand Rapids, Minnesota. Her parents owned the New Grand Theater, where her older sisters, Mary Jane and Virginia, often sang and danced for audiences.

When Judy was two years old, her father took her to his theater to see a young singing group named The Blue Sisters. The three Blue Sisters weren't much older than Judy, and when they took the stage, Judy could barely control herself. She bounced up and down in her seat and clapped excitedly. She looked like she was going to run up the aisle any minute and join them on stage. As soon as the show was over, Judy begged her father to let her sing with her older sisters, but her father said Judy was still too young.

But Judy didn't give up. She spent the next four months pleading with her parents until they finally gave in. Judy would get to sing in the New Grand's Christmas show.

Her parents placed an advertisement in the local paper telling everyone about the show.

"Let's Go to the Grand Show!"
New Grand
(26 December 1924)
Thursday and Friday

Mary Pickford in one of the prettiest pictures she has ever appeared in, entitled "Thru' the Back Door."

A two-reel comedy "Motor Mad" completes the program.

Special for Friday night: the three Gumm children in songs and dances, featuring "Baby Frances", two years of age.

Baby Frances' song
'Jingle Bells'

Judy and her sisters would sing in between movies. Their grandmother even made the long, 85-mile drive along bumpy, back-country roads from Superior, Wisconsin, to see them perform.

When the big night came, Judy's sisters, who were seven and nine years old, took the stage and sang their first number—*When My Sugar Walks Down the Street*, a new jazz song almost no one had heard yet. Halfway through the song, a tiny voice joined them. Mary Jane and Virginia looked around to see who else was singing, then they stepped aside to reveal Judy hiding behind them! The audience laughed and applauded, encouraging Judy to sing. She even did a short tap dance in the middle of the song. She performed two more songs with her sisters before they left the stage to let Judy sing her first solo.

Her mother, Ethel, played piano while Judy belted out *Jingle Bells*, but once Judy got started, she wouldn't stop. Every time the song was supposed to end, she sang, "Jingle Bells, jingle bells" and started the song all over again. She sang it six more times while the audience enjoyed her antics.

Judy's father, however, was desperate to keep the show running on time. It was 9:25—time to start the second movie. Judy's grandmother rushed on stage and grabbed her granddaughter's hand, but Judy fought to keep singing. Finally, her grandmother did the only thing she could do—she picked up Judy, who burst into tears, and carried her away.

Judy threw a fit backstage. She was screaming, "I

want to sing some more!" but her grandmother told her to listen to the audience. They were cheering wildly for two-year-old Judy. And that's when Judy stopped crying. The applause made her feel wonderful. She felt like a star, and she was right.

Judy Garland may have been a little girl, but she was a big talent, and she knew she was going to be a singer forever.

EARLY LIFE

Judy Garland was born on June 10, 1922. It was an exciting time to be in show business. Movie theaters were popping up in nearly every town, hundreds of radio stations were being built, jazz music was sweeping the country, and acts of all kinds were performing on vaudeville stages.

The world didn't know it yet, but in a small, white house in Grand Rapids, Minnesota, one of the greatest entertainers who ever lived was growing up.

Judy Garland's real name was Frances Ethel Gumm. Her name was a combination of her parents' names—Francis (changed to Frances) and Ethel Gumm. Francis, who everybody called Frank, had a beautiful singing voice, while Ethel could play piano, dance, and write music. They met at a theater in Wisconsin in 1913 and quickly formed a musical act featuring Ethel on piano and Frank singing popular songs. A year later, they were married.

In 1915, Ethel gave birth to their first daughter, Mary Jane, and they knew their traveling days were over. They decided to settle down and raise a family, though they continued to perform at local theaters and school functions. Those jobs didn't pay enough to feed their newborn baby, so Frank got a job managing the New Grand Theater. The theater showed both movies and live shows. Frank knew how to draw a crowd, and the New Grand packed them in. Before long, it was the only theater in town.

Frank & Ethel Gumm

Two years later, the Gumms had their second child—Virginia. Frank and Ethel had both been child performers, so it was no surprise that they soon had their daughters singing and dancing in an act called The Gumm Sisters. By the time Virginia was five years old in 1922, they were performing several times a week.

One of the reasons the owners hired Frank to manage the New Grand was that Ethel played piano. Because silent movies didn't have sound, the music during the film was played by a piano player right in the theater!

Then along came Judy. Her father would sing her to sleep with his two favorite songs—the Irish ballad *Danny Boy* and the slave spiritual *Nobody Knows the Trouble I've Seen*. Frank took this last song to heart. He and Ethel were in trouble. His job at the theater didn't pay very much, and they didn't know how they were going to pay for a third child. They only knew that someday "Baby" Gumm would be part of The Gumm Sisters, too.

In September, 1925, less than a year after Judy joined the act in her stunning Christmas debut, she got sick. Her parents rushed her to the nearest hospital more than an hour and a half away. A severe ear infection brought on a high fever, and Judy had to stay in intensive care. At first, her parents worried that Judy might go deaf and never hear music or sing again. As her illness grew worse, they feared she would die.

Fortunately, after a week of doctors sticking tubes in her ear to drain the infection, three-year-old Judy recovered. She couldn't wait to rehearse for the New Grand's upcoming Christmas show. Judy now performed with her sisters all the time, and they soon developed a solid act. Mary Jane and Virginia carried Judy, curled up and hidden in a round hat box, on stage. She would then pop out and do a crazy new dance called The Charleston. It got big laughs and was almost as popular as Judy's singing.

By now, Judy's father owned part of the New Grand Theater. He also wrote articles for the local newspaper. It felt like everybody in town knew and liked the Gumm family, though Judy's favorite thing

The Charleston

8

Judy's house in Grand Rapids, Minnesota

(next to singing on stage) happened right outside her door. The family lived across the street from a candy wagon, where a man sold popcorn, ice cream, caramel apples, licorice and other treats for a penny. Even though the family didn't have a lot of money, Judy's father constantly gave her pennies so she could run across the street and pick out her favorite treat. Judy and her father were very close, and she loved living in Grand Rapids.

But things were about to change for Judy. Her parents were growing tired of small-town life. They dreamed of leaving Minnesota and playing the big theaters in New York City and Chicago. When Judy's father received a letter from an old friend suggesting they try Los Angeles, he loved the idea. He thought his daughters could act in movies. They visited Hollywood, California, just two days before Judy's fourth birthday.

The Gumms immediately toured movie studios to see how films were made. Outside one studio, Frank bumped into Fred Thomson, a silent film cowboy who was one of the biggest movie stars of the day. Frank lied to him and said his daughters were just

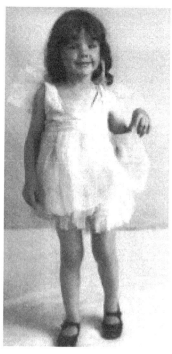

"Baby" Frances, future star

dying to meet him. Fred smiled and led the three Gumm sisters onto the set of his new movie. After seeing this, Frank told his family they were moving to Hollywood to make movies. They packed up everything they owned and four months later returned to California. But they soon discovered that no one becomes a movie star overnight, and four-year-old Judy had a lot of work ahead of her.

Vaudeville

Vaudeville wasn't an actual town—it was a string of towns and cities all across the United States. What made these towns part of vaudeville was that each one had a theater. Vaudeville offered variety shows, with singers, dancers, comedians, magicians, jugglers, acrobats, animal acts, and actors. They were family shows, with **matinee** performances on the weekend. The people who performed in vaudeville were called vaudevillians.

Vaudeville became popular in the 1870s, but died out in the early 1930s because people preferred going to the movies. Also, many big vaudeville stars like Al Jolson, Groucho Marx, and Fanny Brice were making movies and no longer doing live shows. The Gumm Sisters got into vaudeville just as it was ending.

A little-known vaudeville fact: The last performer was often the worst act on the show. His job was to be so bad that the audience would leave. This way, they could clean up the theater for the next show!

HOLLYWOOD, HERE I COME

The Gumm family arrived in Southern California ready to conquer Hollywood. Unfortunately, they found they couldn't afford to live anywhere near Hollywood. Living near movie stars costs a lot of money, so the Gumms moved to a small town named Lancaster in the Mojave (Mo-haav-ee) Desert an hour away. Judy's father then did what he had done in Minnesota—bought a movie theater he hoped to make a big success.

Some people thought Frank was crazy for buying the Valley Theater. How could he fill a big, 500-seat theater when so few people lived in the desert? The residents of Lancaster, mostly cowboys and railroad workers, worried that Frank could never sell enough tickets to stay in business, but Frank had a trick up his sleeve: three talented daughters he just knew audiences would love.

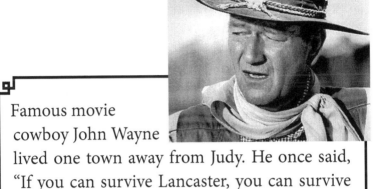

Famous movie cowboy John Wayne lived one town away from Judy. He once said, "If you can survive Lancaster, you can survive anything." It was a rough place to live!

The Gumm Sisters took the stage the day after Frank bought the theater. People enjoyed Judy's silly dancing, but they were **mesmerized** by her singing. Within a few days, word spread around Lancaster and the neighboring towns that people just had to go see the sensational Baby Gumm. In fact, the Valley Theater usually made the most money on the nights Judy sang. Within a few months, The Gumm Sisters were performing at restaurants, schools, and private clubs. Judy's mother even packed a fold-out stage in her car so Judy could perform anywhere they went. Then she would pull out the stage for her daughter to give a quick fifteen-minute show.

Ethel decided it was time to get serious about her daughters' careers. She knew performing in restaurants in the desert would never lead to movie roles, so when Judy was six years old, she visited a brand new dance studio in Hollywood run by Ethel Meglin. Ms. Meglin had been a dancer in several movies and gave dance lessons right on the lot of Keystone Studios. Director Mack Sennett, who had discovered the great comedian Charlie Chaplin and created the Keystone Cops, urged Ms. Meglin to teach dance. He even donated a building for her studio. He hoped to recruit talented children for his movies.

Judy's mother was convinced that this dance studio was the one to get her daughters movie jobs, and she desperately tried to sign them up. There was only one problem: she didn't have enough money.

That's when the two Ethels made a deal. Judy's mother would play piano for free at The Meglin Professional Children's School if Ms. Meglin taught her daughters to dance. Soon Judy and her sisters were making the hour-long trip to Los Angeles twice a week to learn complicated dance steps. No longer would The Gumm Sisters rely only on raw talent—they'd be trained dancers!

Within months, all their hard work began to pay off. Ethel Meglin put together a dance troupe called Meglin's Kiddies. She booked them into theaters all over Los Angeles. The Gumm Sisters usually danced for one song, and then sang one or two more. Judy's mother hoped a Hollywood talent scout would put them in movies, but that didn't happen. Instead, they found a new way to entertain people.

Ms. Meglin started an afternoon radio show. She put Judy and her sisters on every Wednesday afternoon for fifteen minutes as part of *The Kiddies' Hour*. They told jokes, made up stories, and sang for listeners all over Southern California. The Gumm Sisters were among the most popular acts on the show and started getting fan mail. Lots of fan mail. They even got one letter from movie star William S. Hart asking them to sing his favorite song!

But no one put them in the movies.

No one, that is, until Ethel Meglin came through again. Meglin's Kiddies would star in their own movie. Filming started the day after Judy's seventh birthday. Two days later, filming was done. The movie was eighteen straight minutes of singing, dancing, and gymnastics. *The Big Revue* starred Ethel Meglin's Famous Hollywood Wonder Kids. It didn't matter that none of them were famous yet—Ms. Meglin was sure they would be. And she had a big surprise for Judy. Since The Gumm Sisters were her best performers, she gave them a number to sing all by themselves.

A tiny member of Meglin's Kiddies introduced them, and then the trio launched into the jazz song *That's the Good Old Sunny South.** The Gumm Sisters were the only act to have their name listed in the movie.

Judy was excited. The film debuted at a big theater in Los Angeles, and then was sent to theaters all over the United States. Judy told everyone she was going to be a movie star.

But that didn't happen. Although Judy quickly landed parts in three other movie shorts as part of a troupe named The Vitaphone Kiddies, she wasn't exactly a star. In *The Wedding of Jack & Jill*, another actress played Jill, while Judy sang one song with her sisters and another one solo. The best of these films was the last one, *Bubbles*, which was in color rather than black and white—something very rare in 1930

See all scenes marked * at *johnbriggsbooks.net*!

The Gumm Sisters in The Big Revue (left to right: Judy, Virginia, and Mary Jane

—but Judy was disappointed. Her big scene was only a two-line solo in one song. Judy's mother was getting frustrated, too. Unlike their first film, The Gumm Sisters didn't even get their name listed in the credits.

Determined to get her children bigger parts in the movies, Judy's mother arranged an audition for them in the fall of 1929 at Metro-Goldwyn-Mayer, the biggest studio in Hollywood. Judy sang her heart out for a director, but he wasn't impressed and passed on The Gumm Sisters. They would have to look for another way to break into feature films.

Judy's movie career had stalled, but the news was far worse. In October, 1929, the country fell into the Great Depression. Many people were suddenly poor. Banks and factories

Acts Featuring Judy Garland

The Gumm Sisters (sometimes called The Gumdrops) (1924-1935)

Meglin's Kiddies (1929-1930)

The Vitaphone Kiddies (1929-1930)

The Hollywood Starlets Trio (1929-1930)

closed their doors. One in four people didn't have a job. People worried about buying food and having a place to live. This meant that many people stopped going to the theater. Fortunately, Judy and her sisters were still getting paid to be on the radio. They now had their own show called *The Hollywood Starlets Trio.* Unlike *The Kiddies Hour,* this one included their mother playing piano and conducting the orchestra. The Gumm Sisters also performed in any theater that would book them just to keep food on the family's table.

The Great Depression

The Great Depression lasted from 1929 until the late 1930s. On October 29, 1929 (a day known as Black Tuesday), the New York Stock Exchange "crashed." The stock market is a place where people buy part of a company. The crash wiped out many family fortunes.

Some banks lost all their money in the stock market, too. Factories and businesses laid off workers because they couldn't pay them. Twenty-five percent of the people were unemployed. Many begged for food.

In 1933, Franklin D. Roosevelt became president. He created programs to get people working again. It took several more years, but eventually the Great Depression came to an end.

Homeless people built shelters in parks called Hooverville, named after Herbert Hoover, the president when the Great Depression began.

The Valley Theater was struggling to stay in business. The Gumms were so poor that they had to live in their car. Judy's parents were fighting all the time and eventually separated. Ethel moved to Los Angeles with her daughters to keep them close to Hollywood while Frank stayed in Lancaster to run the movie theater. Judy was extremely upset and cried often. She missed her father, and though he visited when he could, it was not often enough for Judy. It seemed the only place she was truly happy was on stage.

While in Los Angeles, Judy had to go to a new school: the Lawlor School for Professional Children. But Ma Lawlor's was no ordinary school. Although students learned math and reading, they were all performers, and a few, like Baby Peggy (who was now thirteen years old and no longer a baby), were already movie stars. Judy was a bit nervous about going to a new school. She may have been extremely outgoing on stage, but she acted shy around kids she didn't know. On the first day of school, Ma Lawlor asked Judy to introduce herself by singing a song. Most students would have been scared, but nine-year-old Judy was thrilled. She broke into a **rendition** of *Blue Moon* that blew her new classmates away. It turned out Judy would much rather sing to the class than get up in front of them and talk.

One other big event happened that first day—Judy met ten-year-old Mickey Rooney. Mickey, like Baby Peggy, was a movie star. He went up to Judy that morning and told her he had seen The Gumm Sisters perform a year ago and thought she was terrific. Judy said, "Do you really think so?" and Mickey said he did.

On her first day at a new school, Judy met the person who would be her best friend for the rest of her life.

Mickey Rooney and Judy Garland

By 1931, Judy was no longer in the movies. She and her sisters failed another audition, this time at Universal Studios. Fortunately, Judy loved being in front of a live audience. The applause was the one thing that made her feel happy and forget her troubles.

"Come on, get happy
Chase all your cares away."
From *Get Happy***, one of Judy's best-known songs

Then, in 1932, Hollywood changed forever. One of Ethel Meglin's Kiddies, a little girl with strawberry curls, appeared in her first movie. Within two years, six-year-old Shirley Temple was the biggest movie star in the world. Studios rushed to find children for their movies, hoping they would find the next "Shirley Temple."

Judy went on more auditions, but the results were always the same. Producers thought that Judy was either too old or not cute enough. Finally, her mother decided that if Hollywood didn't want her daughters, she'd take them out of Hollywood. She was going to have her daughters perform all over the

Hear all songs marked ** at *johnbriggsbooks.net*!

United States, just like she had wanted to do when she was younger. At last The Gumm Sisters would be a full part of vaudeville.

Judy was going on the road.

Shirley Temple

Shirley Temple was just three years old when she appeared in her first film. Two years later she began a movie career that few actors will ever match. From 1935-1938 she was the top box office star in the world. Nobody's movies made more money than hers.

She could sing and dance, and made songs like *On the Good Ship Lollipop* and *Animal Crackers in My Soup* famous. She won a Juvenile Academy Award when she was just seven years old. Girls everywhere dressed like her and bought Shirley Temple dolls and toys. A man at a restaurant in Los Angeles even invented a drink for her. More than eighty years later, people still drink a Shirley Temple!

Shirley Temple (continued)

When Shirley retired from acting in 1964, she ran for a seat in the United States Congress, but lost. She later became the U.S. ambassador to two countries. She also worked for the United Nations, promoting peace in different countries. She even tried to save wild animals. Shirley died in 2014 at the age of eighty-five.

Shirley's mother did her daughter's hair for every movie to make sure she had exactly 52 curls.

Some people thought Shirley was really a tiny adult pretending to be a child because they believed no one so young could be so talented!

FROM GUMM TO GARLAND

The 36th World's Fair came to Chicago in 1933. This wasn't a small county fair with a few rides and games, but a giant fair that lasted for more than a year. More than forty-eight million people from around the world came to see the exhibits, including a futuristic home with a personal helicopter pad, a giant blimp, the first Major League Baseball All-Star game, and a camp set up to look like an African safari. Ethel Gumm wanted her daughters to be part of it, so she contacted several theaters. The Old Mexico Cabaret hired them to perform for four weeks in the summer of 1934.

Ethel took $400 out of the bank to pay for their

trip. She also arranged for her daughters to perform at several theaters in Colorado to earn extra money along the way. Everything started out well for the sisters. When they reached Chicago, they were allowed to perform a few songs at various theaters in the city, as well as at the fair. Judy was quickly spotted by World's Fair officials and made the "guest of honor" at the fair's Eighth Children's Day. This meant she got to sing in front of thousands of people throughout the day.

The official name of the Chicago World's Fair was *A Century of Progress*. It showcased inventions designed to make the world better. It was nicknamed The Rainbow Fair because it portrayed the future as a bright and happy place!

After impressing audiences at the fair, The Gumm Sisters expected people to flock to the Old Mexico Cabaret to see them, but the theater was struggling. During their second week of shows, the owner closed the theater and refused to pay them. Most of the Gumm's $400 was gone, and they were counting on this money to pay for food. Ethel kept asking the owner for the money, until he told her that if she didn't stop bothering him, she'd wind up "at the bottom of Lake Michigan." He meant that if she didn't go away, he'd throw her in the lake and drown her. Ethel took the threat seriously. In the 1930s, Chicago was a city run by gangsters, and Ethel believed the owner actually knew somebody who would kill her.

By now, the Gumms had been on the road for more than a month and didn't have enough money to get back to California. They went from theater to theater looking for work, but no one was hiring— at least not until Mary Jane's boyfriend heard that one of Chicago's best theaters was looking for an act to "fill out the bill." Judy and her sisters gratefully accepted a four-week engagement at the Oriental Theater in August, 1934.

Comedian, actor, and radio star George "Georgie" Jessel hosted the show. George instantly liked the girls, but because he had never heard of them, he made them one of the opening acts. He then watched them on the first night to see if they were any good. And were they ever! He was amazed that Judy's voice was so powerful she didn't need a microphone to reach the back row. Everyone in the theater could hear her. He thought people on the street could probably hear her. And so, after just one show,

George moved them up to the next-to-last spot, putting the weaker acts on before them. He knew The Gumm Sisters were a hard act to follow.

Then came the show where the sisters found out it could be hard to follow George Jessel.

George was always joking around. He used to tell audiences that the littlest Gumm sister could make you "tingle, laugh or cry whether her name was Frances Gumm, Minnie Ha-Ha or Algrena Handelplotz." But one night when he introduced The Gumm Sisters, the audience laughed at their name. They thought George was making it up. He hadn't meant it as a joke, but as he often noted on stage, the name sounded funny. After the show, he told The Gumm Sisters they really should change their name.

"To what?" they asked.

George didn't know, but since he had suggested it, he felt he needed to come up with an answer. According to legend, he took a few seconds to think about it and said, "Garland, because you're as pretty as a garland of flowers." The truth is that he took time to think about it. Several months, in fact. That's when he suggested they name themselves after one of his best friends, theater critic Robert Garland.

The sisters loved it. They were so excited about changing their last name that they changed their

Judy at the Chicago World's Fair

first names, too. Although Virginia (whose first name was really Dorothy) kept the nickname Jimmy, Mary Jane became Suzy and Frances "Baby" Gumm became Judy. She took her name from the popular song *Judy* that went, "If you think she's a saint and you find out she ain't, that's Judy."

The act was set. The Gumm Sisters were now The Garland Sisters, and they were ready to return Hollywood. And it turned out Hollywood was finally ready for them.

The Gumm Sisters had always had problems with their name. One theater even listed them as "The Glum Sisters." Now that's a depressing act!

A few months after heading home to California, The Garland Sisters got a second audition at Universal Studios, and all that time spent performing on the road made them better. Universal signed the girls to a one-picture deal for a movie called *The Great Ziegfeld* about the founder of *The Ziegfeld Follies*, Florenz Ziegfeld. Judy couldn't believe it. She would be in a movie about the man who hired her dance teacher, Ethel Meglin, for several of his own films. He had died three years earlier and Universal had big plans for the movie.

Unfortunately, the executives at Universal changed their minds and sold the movie to MGM, and just like that, Judy and her sisters were out of the picture. Universal then decided they didn't want The Garland Sisters either and released them from their contract. Once again, Judy failed to land a movie role from a major studio.

Two and a half months later, Judy got another shot at the big time. The Garland Sisters were back singing in movie theaters between films when a record producer caught their act. On the way home with his wife, he couldn't stop talking about them, particularly Judy. The next day he went back to the theater and watched them four more times. He couldn't wait to get them into a sound studio and make a record.

He contacted Decca Records headquarters in New York City to let them know he had a future star on his hands. The Garland Sisters recorded one song while their mother played piano, then Judy sang two more by herself. One of the songs she performed was *On the Good Ship Lollipop*** made famous by fellow Meglin Kiddie Shirley Temple. The record producer hoped it would be a hit for Judy, too, but for some reason, his bosses in New York decided not to offer her a contract. The records were never released.

For the second time in three months, Judy had been turned down.

Not only were the records never released, no one heard them for another twenty-five years until the audition tapes were found in a trash can outside Judy's house. Apparently she threw them away!

Judy's mother once again decided it was time to take her daughters on the road. If Hollywood didn't fully appreciate her daughters' talent, she knew live audiences did. In July, she took them to Lake Tahoe,

California, to perform for tourists. After nearly two weeks of singing and dancing, it was time to go home, but on the way back to Los Angeles, the girls realized they left several of their hats behind. When they returned to the hotel, Judy raced inside to grab them. The owner of the hotel saw her and waved her over. He asked her to sing for two friends of his. Judy quickly belted out the song *Dinah*.

"Dinah
Is there anyone finer
In the state of Carolina?"
Lyrics from *Dinah* (1925)

The owners' two friends were songwriter Lew Brown and his agent, Al Rosen. Al wasted no time giving Judy's mother his phone number. He told her to call him when they returned to Los Angeles. He was interested in representing the sisters and sending them on movie auditions.

This may have been the best thing that happened to Judy in Lake Tahoe, but it wasn't the best thing to happen to Mary Jane. While performing at the hotel, Judy introduced her nineteen-year-old sister to a musician named Lee Kahn. A few weeks later, in August, 1935, they were married. Mary Jane then made another big announcement: she was leaving the act. It looked like The Garland Sisters would be a duo with Jimmy and Judy—at least until eighteen-year-old Jimmy announced she was leaving, too. She had been tired of performing for several years and only stuck with it because they were a trio and the family needed the money. Now that Mary Jane was leaving, she saw no reason to stay.

Thirteen-year-old Judy had been performing with her sisters since she was two. Even though she was the star of their act, they had always worked together, doing hundreds of live shows and radio appearances as a trio, but now, overnight, she was a solo act.

Judy realized she could either quit performing or pursue her dream. She decided that just because her sisters quit showbiz didn't mean she had to. She was still determined to become a movie star, this time on her own.

WHAT TO DO WITH JUDY?

Nine months after MGM removed Judy and her sisters from *The Great Ziegfeld*, they decided to give Judy another chance. She would get to audition in front of several of MGM's top producers.

Unfortunately, the audition started out terribly.

Judy's mother couldn't take her to the audition, so her father went instead. He played piano while Judy sang *Zing! Went the Strings of My Heart*—but unlike Ethel, Frank was a terrible piano player. MGM executives talked it over and decided they liked Judy's voice enough to give her another chance. They asked a man named Roger Edens to take over for Frank and play the song again.

When Judy finished, no one said anything. Judy was nervous. She didn't know if she passed the audition. The men simply said, "Thank you" and went away. Three days later, MGM boss Louis (Loo-ee) B. Mayer ordered a contract for Judy. It turned out he was so sure he had something special in her that he didn't even ask for a screen test to see how she looked on film. He wanted her to work for MGM. Just two weeks after her audition, Judy signed the contract. She would be an actress at the biggest studio in Hollywood!

It was a seven-year deal. They would pay Judy $100 per week at a time when most people only made $30 per week. Roger Edens became her voice coach, and he wasted no time putting Judy to work. On her first day on the MGM lot, he gave her singing lessons, hoping to make her already amazing voice even better.

As much as the executives at MGM admired Judy's talent, they weren't sure what to do with her. At thirteen, she was too old to be a child star and too young for grown-up movies. Several producers thought she was too short to be in pictures, and some even worried she wasn't pretty enough. In fact, Louis B. Mayer teased Judy whenever he saw her by calling her, "My little hunchback."

Judy's first day at MGM

That's when the bosses at MGM put Judy in the one place no one could see her: the radio. They arranged for her to appear on a National Broadcasting Company (NBC) program called T*he Shell* **Chateau** (Sha-tow) *Hour.*

Judy's first appearance went well, and the host took a liking to her. A few weeks later he invited her to come back on his show, but Judy's second visit came at a very bad time. Just hours before she was supposed to go on the air, her father was rushed to the hospital with an infection in his spine. The family hurriedly set up a radio in his hospital room while the nurses worked hard to bring down his fever. Judy spent some time visiting her father, then left for the radio station, promising to see him the next day.

Judy decided to sing the song from her audition, the one her father tried so hard to play on the piano. Her voice sounded strained and sad as she worked through *Zing! Went the Strings of My Heart.*** It was clear that she was thinking of her father as she sang the words:

> *Your eyes made skies seem blue again*
> *What else could I do again*
> *But keep repeating through and through*
> *"I love you, love you"*

Frank smiled as Judy's voice reached him through the tiny speakers. He knew she was singing about him. Despite his improved spirits, the infection got worse and in the middle of the night, Frank Gumm passed away.

Judy never got to see her father again.

Judy was devastated, later calling it "The worst day

of my life." The pain was far worse than any failed audition. Her father had been her mentor, the person from whom she inherited her wonderful voice. Judy dedicated herself to carrying on her family's showbiz tradition and becoming the star her father never did.

Less than two weeks after Judy's second *Shell Chateau Hour*, the show's orchestra leader and conductor, Victor Young, called her. He didn't want Judy back on the show—at least not yet. Young had a second job as the music director for Decca Records, and he wanted to get Judy in the studio for a second audition, this time with his full support.

Judy arrived at the studio just as Ginger Rogers was finishing a recording session. Ginger Rogers was one of the most famous dancers in Hollywood, but she also sang. On this day, Ginger finished early, so Victor Young sent Judy in to sing with the same orchestra. He even conducted it himself, working with Judy like he had on the radio. Judy's two songs bowled over the bosses at Decca, and although they didn't sign her to a record contract, they did agree to let her come back into the studio to sing several more songs. This turned out to be a shrewd move because seven months later, in the summer of 1936, Judy recorded two songs at Decca's studios in New York. Just two days after Judy's fourteenth birthday, she had her first hit records, *Swing Mr. Charlie* and the popular jazz tune from Benny Goodman, *Stompin' at the Savoy.***

Lost for Good

Judy's audition tapes for Decca Records were never released to the public. In 1943, they were donated to the scrap metal drive to make items for World War II. No copies were ever made.

Although Judy was now a radio star, her movie career had stopped. After nearly a year, she had yet to make a film for MGM. Not knowing what to do with her, they loaned her out to another big studio, 20th Century-Fox. Loaning out an actor meant one studio paid another to "borrow" or use their actors. This was a standard part of the old Hollywood studio system.

20th Century-Fox gave Judy the role of the little sister in *Pigskin Parade*, a film about a smalltime college football team invited to play in a big game. Judy got rave reviews, particularly for her **sentimental** performance of *It's Love I'm After.**

MGM realized they made a mistake in loaning Judy out to another studio and never did it again. They knew they had to find a film for her.

The Studio System

During the Golden Age of Hollywood (1927-1948), the five major studios and three smaller studios controlled almost every aspect of an actor's life. They taught them to act, decided what movies they would be in, what color their hair would be, and what clothes they would wear. Studios could change an actor's name and even life story if they wanted to.

By 1948, the studio system was coming to a close. The United States government limited the power of movie studios. Also, many film stars wanted to choose for themselves what films to be in, while small movie studios (called independents) and television networks were cutting into the big studios' profits. By 1960, the studio system was almost dead. The last studio-system actress was signed in 1974, almost fifty years after it began.

In *Pigskin Parade*, actor Jack Haley played the football coach. At one point in the film he does something he shouldn't have and says, "If I only had a brain." Three years later, he would play the Tin Man in *The Wizard of Oz*, where he would listen to the Scarecrow say, "If I only had a brain," while he went looking for a heart!

MGM quickly threw Judy in a short film co-starring Deanna Durbin, her chief rival for acting parts at the studio. As producers struggled to find a feature film for Judy, she made the decision easy for them. In February, 1937, she was invited to sing at Clark Gable's birthday party. He was one of MGM's biggest stars, and the studio threw him a giant party. Fourteen-year-old Judy was a little nervous singing for him, but no one knew it from her performance. Judy belted out a sweet-but-funny version of *(Dear Mr. Gable) You Made Me Love You*.

"You made me love you
I didn't want to do it, I didn't want to do it
You made me love you"

Clark Gable loved it. He gave Judy a big hug and cut her a slice of cake. He then spent time showing her around the set. Judy's performance was all anyone at the party could talk about.

MGM executives were excited, too. They were getting ready to shoot a movie called *Broadway Melodies of 1938* and gave Judy a part singing to Clark Gable. Of course, the real Clark Gable wasn't available, so she sang *You Made Me Love You* to his picture.* The scene was the highlight of the film and a big hit with moviegoers.

It looked like Judy had finally "arrived" in Hollywood, but now MGM was worried that Judy would be just a singer in films and not a full-fledged actress. They needed to find a way to keep her working in feature films. And that's when Judy got another big break.

Her best friend, Mickey Rooney, had become the first teenage movie star. He was making big-budget films like *Captains Courageous* and *Little Lord Fauntleroy*, but it was his plucky performance as Andy Hardy that made him famous. The Andy Hardy movies focused on a teenage boy looking to date "the prettiest girl in town." The films were immensely popular with adults and teens alike.

MGM quickly added Judy to the series. She had

*Clark Gable giving Judy a "thank you" hug
at his birthday party*

done one other movie with Mickey in 1938, the
exciting horse-racing film *Thoroughbreds Don't Cry*,
and studio bosses noticed two things: Judy and

Mickey liked each other, and they were about the same height: short. Mickey was only three inches taller than 4'11" Judy, and they looked like they belonged together. MGM executives also thought that Judy's "plain" looks made her perfect to play the girl next door who develops a crush on the older Andy. Audiences liked the pairing of the happy-go-lucky Andy and the lovelorn Betsy, and Judy did two more Andy Hardy movies before leaving the series.

Judy's career was finally in full swing. Her records were being played all over the radio, and she was appearing in two or three movies per year. That's when MGM made a huge announcement: they were remaking the classic *The Wonderful Wizard of Oz*. The movie had already been made three times, but never in color and never with the kind of talent MGM was putting together. They were turning L. Frank Baum's book about a Kansas farm girl trapped in a magical land into a major spectacle, complete with Munchkins, flying monkeys, an Emerald City, and a cast of top-flight dancers and singers. Judy desperately wanted to be a part of it because everyone was saying it would be one of MGM's biggest films of 1939.

Then Judy got the bad news. The producer didn't want her to play Dorothy. He had already offered the part to Shirley Temple.

It looked like Judy would have to keep doing small films for MGM unless she could get another big break.

Judy and Mickey in Love Finds Andy Hardy (1938)

THERE'S NO PLACE LIKE HOLLYWOOD

Shirley Temple was so sure she would play Dorothy in *The Wizard of Oz* that she joked to reporters that, "There's no place like home." And Shirley had every right to believe she was a shoo-in for the part. She was one of the world's most famous movie stars and close to Dorothy's age in the books, but behind the scenes, things were not going well for Shirley. Roger Edens was not impressed by Shirley's singing, particularly on the first song, *Over the Rainbow*. He felt that nine-year-old Shirley's voice wasn't strong enough to make the song truly special. He recommended that she not be offered the part.

Before MGM could find a polite way to announce that Shirley Temple would not be playing Dorothy, 20th Century-Fox declared it was not loaning out its biggest star.

With Shirley Temple gone from *The Wizard of Oz*, Judy was an obvious choice to play Dorothy. It was no secret in Hollywood that songwriters Harold Arlen and Yip Harburg wrote *Over the Rainbow* for Judy, but producers turned to Deanna Durbin instead. Deanna had been let go by MGM, but she was now a big star at Universal, and unlike Shirley Temple, Deanna had a beautiful voice. This posed a surprising problem for the filmmakers. In the original script, Dorothy entered a singing contest. The actress she was supposed to compete against had already been hired, and she had a voice like an opera singer—just like Deanna. Roger Edens convinced the producers they had to go in another direction and find someone with the rhythm and flexibility of a jazz singer. And so they did. In late February, 1938, MGM announced that they had found the perfect actress to play Dorothy: their very own Judy Garland!

Although Judy now had the part, filming didn't start right away. There were major problems with the script. Writers were always being hired and fired

Before filming began, fourteen writers had worked on the story.

Casting Problems

It wasn't just hard to cast Dorothy. Actor Buddy Ebsen was so allergic to the silver powder they used to make him look like the Tin Man that he could barely breathe. He had to be placed inside an "iron lung" to save his life. Jack Haley soon replaced him as the Tin Man. The good news is that Ebsen would become famous twenty years later as the star of the TV show *The Beverly Hillbillies,,*

An iron lung

Even with all the delays, Judy didn't stay idle. That summer, she starred in her second film with Mickey Rooney, *Love Finds Andy Hardy*, considered one of the best Andy Hardy films. Judy's Hollywood star kept rising, though she was still playing second fiddle to Mickey Rooney.

Finally, near the end of August, 1938, producers brought Judy in for costume fittings. They wanted to make the sixteen-year-old starlet look younger than she was. The director put her in a curly blond wig and told her to act cute, like Shirley Temple. Eleven days later, that director was fired and all of his film destroyed. He was quickly replaced by George Cukor, who removed the wig and ordered Judy to act like a "girl from Kansas." He let her look and act her age, but lightened her hair to make it a soft brown. He also changed the costumes of the Scarecrow and the Wicked Witch, giving them the look we know today. Unfortunately, George didn't want to stay with the picture. After only a few days he left to direct MGM's other big film that year, *Gone With the Wind* starring Clark Gable.

At last, producers settled on letting Victor Fleming direct. Although Fleming had never directed a musical, he was known for getting movies done on time and without spending too much money. He also had a good reputation for working with large casts and even larger sets.

Make-Up Troubles

Judy wasn't the only one to have make-up problems on the set of *The Wizard of Oz*. The Scarecrow's mask was glued to actor Ray Bolger's face, which left dark lines on his skin for the rest of his life. And the make-up used to create the Wicked Witch's green face contained copper. Copper is so poisonous that actress Margaret Hamilton wasn't allowed to touch food while wearing it. She had to be fed by an assistant. She also had to stay late whenever she worked so that the make-up people could remove every last pinch of green powder from her face and hands to keep her safe.

While Judy's scenes went well, other actors weren't so lucky. Poor Toto got stepped on and couldn't work for several days. A wire snapped and sent a flying monkey crashing to the floor. Fortunately, the little person playing the monkey wasn't seriously hurt.

The Wicked Witch's stunt double was sitting on the flying broomstick—which was really a pipe with smoke coming out of it—when it exploded. She ended up with permanent scars on her legs. The worst accident, though, happened to The Wicked Witch. When she disappeared from Munchkinland in a giant puff of smoke, one of the fire props went off too soon, badly burning her. The make-up assistant rushed onto the set to scrub the copper-based powder from Margaret Hamilton's face. Her quick thinking is the only thing that kept Margaret from being permanently disfigured by the melting toxin. Margaret was rushed to the hospital and couldn't work on *The Wizard of Oz* for four months.

One major problem all the actors faced was the extremely hot lights. Because the scenes in Oz were shot in Technicolor, a brand new technology, the lights had to be hotter than normal movie lights. This made the actors sweat heavily in their costumes. Filming constantly had to be stopped to give the actors water and fix running make-up. Filming was slow, but within three months, the actors had shot all the scenes in Oz.

That's when the film lost another director. For the second time, Victor Fleming was taking over for George Cukor, this time after Cukor was fired from

Gone With the Wind. The director who replaced Fleming was known mostly for his work in silent films and gave the black and white scenes in Kansas a dark quality to contrast them with the bright colors of Oz. One of the last scenes he shot was Judy singing *Over the Rainbow**.

Weird but True Wizard Fact

The suit coat worn by the Wizard was bought at a used clothing store. It turned out that it was donated by none other than L. Frank Baum, the man who wrote *The Wizard of Oz!*

Over the next three months, editors put the film together. When MGM studio bosses saw it, they liked it, but they had one request: remove *Over the Rainbow* from the film. They thought it slowed down the movie. One of the producers flatly refused saying, "If that song goes, I go, too!" To keep him happy, MGM made two versions of the movie, one with and one without *Over the Rainbow.* Test audiences overwhelmingly preferred the one with, and the song stayed in the picture.

Finally the film was ready for paying customers.

While most movies were shown first in New York City or Los Angeles, MGM decided to do something different. Since the story revolved around a girl from the Midwest, they opted to show it there first. However, they didn't choose Kansas. For some strange reason they picked a tiny town in Wisconsin, the state where Judy's parents met twenty-eight years before. People left the theater saying they loved the film, and two weeks later, *The Wizard of Oz* was released to theaters all over the country. Audiences and critics loved the movie, but good reviews did not mean good **revenue**, and the film was a box-office failure. It barely made enough money to pay for its budget. Still, the news wasn't all bad. The following February, the film was nominated for six Academy Awards (also known as the Oscars), including Best Picture. It lost to *Gone With the Wind*, but it won Best Music for *Over the Rainbow*. Plus, earlier that night, Judy got the best news of her career so far. Mickey Rooney, the top box office star of 1939, walked on stage and announced that "Miss Judy Garland" had won the Juvenile Academy Award for best performance by a child actor.* She let out a squeal as her best friend handed her the gold statue. He kissed her on the cheek and said, "How about doing us all a little favor now and singing *Over the*

Rainbow?" but Judy was gushing and nearly speechless. As the orchestra played the opening notes, she smoothed out her dress, composed herself, and launched into a soulful rendition of the song. There was no doubt about it now—Judy was a major star, and after several years of giving her small parts, MGM finally came up with a new plan: put Judy in as many movies as possible.

Judy called her Juvenile Academy Award her "Munchkin statue" because it was smaller than a regular Oscar!

LIVING LIKE A MOVIE STAR

Four months after Judy won the Juvenile Academy Award for *The Wizard of Oz*, two big things happened in her life: she graduated from Hollywood High School, and MGM gave her a movie-star-sized contract, raising her pay from to $2,000 per week!

Judy had her own ideas on how to be more grown-up, too. In July, 1941, a month after her nineteenth birthday, Judy married musician and composer David Rose. The couple planned a big wedding, but in the end, kept it small, with only Judy's mother and stepfather in attendance. Judy hadn't talked much to her mother since her father died, but thought she should be at her wedding. Although David and Judy loved talking about music, the marriage wasn't a happy one, and they divorced after three years. Judy never recorded any of his music.

David Rose

David Rose was a very successful film composer. He was nominated for two Oscars and nine Emmys, winning the Emmy four times!

In 1941, Judy had one of her showbiz dreams come true—she would get to copy the life of her dance teacher, Ethel Meglin, by starring in the film *Ziegfeld Girl*. Although Judy had been fired from *The Great Ziegfeld* four years before, MGM wasn't taking her out of this one. Producers gave Judy second billing in the film, ahead of rival Lana Turner. Even though they had gone to Ma Lawlor's school together, they were not good friends. In the movie *Love Finds Andy Hardy*, Judy's character is jealous of Lana's character when Andy falls for her, and the same was true in real life. Judy always felt she wasn't as pretty as Lana, and Lana enjoyed stealing Judy's boyfriends. Being listed ahead of Lana in the movie was a huge triumph!

Life Imitates Art

Just like her character in the Andy Hardy films, Judy had a crush on Mickey Rooney. They never dated because, as Judy said, "He liked other girls." One of those girls was Lana Turner. They dated in 1939. Judy and Lana eventually became friends since Judy admired Lana's beauty and Lana loved Judy's talent. In the 1950s, they were next-door neighbors!

Ziegfeld Girl wasn't a hit for MGM, but there were bigger problems on the horizon. On December 7, 1941, Japan attacked the United States at the Pearl Harbor naval base in Hawaii. America entered World War II, and Hollywood did its part. Many of Judy's friends, including Clark Gable and *Ziegfeld Girl* costar James Stewart, went to war. Judy spent the next several years trying to improve soldier **morale**.

Judy recorded songs specifically for soldiers serving in Europe, Africa, and Asia. In 1943, she appeared in the short film *Strictly G.I.* to sing *Over the Rainbow* after a soldier wrote a letter asking her to. The USO, or United Service Organizations, sent Judy all over the country. She traveled more than 100,000 miles to entertain the troops. Perhaps the strangest thing that happened to Judy came just three weeks after Pearl Harbor. The soldiers at Fort Ord, California, made her an **honorary** military cop!

By 1944, however, Judy was growing unhappy with her career. Film critics disliked many of her movies, including *Presenting Lily Mars* and *Girl Crazy*. Judy knew she needed to turn things around if she wanted to keep working.

Judy and Mickey have a laugh with soldiers after a USO show.

She was offered the starring role in a new musical, *Meet Me in St. Louis* (Loo-ee). It would be the first Technicolor film for Judy since *The Wizard of Oz*, but there were major problems with the picture. The script had to go through several rewrites, just like *Oz*, and the two men hired to write the music had never worked in movies. Even the director, Vincente Minnelli, had only made two films, and neither was a success. Judy worried this would be another flop, and she arranged a meeting with Vincente to talk him into quitting. It didn't work. Vincente was new to movies, but as a Broadway director, he knew how to make musicals. Judy was not convinced and often made fun of Vincente in front of the cast and crew—until she saw herself on film. Judy couldn't believe how beautiful Vincente made her look. From that moment on, she gave him her full co-operation. Of course, Vincente may have had good reason for making Judy look good: he had fallen in love with her. Judy didn't know it yet, but she had met her second husband.

When *Meet Me in St. Louis* was released nationwide in January 1945, it was an instant hit with critics and fans alike. It received five Oscar nominations, with Margaret O'Brien winning a Juvenile Academy Award for her role as little sister Tootie. Judy also scored three hit songs from the movie, two of which—*The Trolley Song* and *Have Yourself a Merry Little Christmas*—are listed among the top 100 movie songs of all time. Judy was the first person to record *Have Yourself a Merry Little Christmas**, and her sad, soulful voice made it an instant holiday classic. Seven decades later, it is still played by radio stations and shopping centers everywhere.

Judy was back on top of the movie world!

Judy and Vincente married in 1945, just five days after her 23rd birthday. Louis B. Mayer stepped in

Judy holds up baby Liza

for Judy's father and gave the bride away. Less than a year later, she gave birth to a daughter, Liza.

Raising a bouncing baby girl might keep most people busy, but Judy was still cranking out big hits like *The Harvey Girls* and *Ziegfeld Follies*. Her rendition of *On the Atchison, Topeka, and the Santa Fe* in

The Harvey Girls won the Oscar for Best Song. Judy's career was on a roll, and once again MGM offered her more money: $6,000 a week. That's $80,000 a week today, or $4 million per year! Judy happily accepted the five-year contract because she didn't want to make movies anywhere else.

All that was about to change.

Judy managed another hit for MGM with *Easter Parade*, the biggest moneymaker of 1948. Legendary dancer Fred Astaire came out of retirement just to work with Judy, and Judy would later list it as her favorite film. By now, however, a dark secret had taken over Judy's life. She was addicted to drugs. When she was a teenager, MGM doctors gave Judy pills because she had to get up so early (sometimes

On the Atchison, Topeka, and the Santa Fe

The Atchison, Topeka, and the Santa Fe was actually a railroad that connected twelve states from California to Illinois. Judy Garland first sang the song for Decca Records in 1945 after she and Vincente rode on the Santa Fe Super Chief on their honeymoon!

before dawn after only four hours of sleep) and stay on set till late at night. Judy took a pill to wake up and sometimes more pills to stay awake. At night, she took another pill to go to sleep. Soon, Judy was taking these drugs all the time, and they were ruining her life. She became unpredictable and often didn't show up for filming. When Judy collapsed while making *Annie Get Your Gun* in 1949, she sought help from a hospital to overcome her addiction. After six weeks, Judy left the hospital and felt ready to return to work, but Louis B. Mayer wasn't so sure. He didn't know if he could trust her. It took four months before he let Judy on a film set.

In October, 1949, Judy started rehearsing dance numbers for the movie *Summer Stock*. The pressure proved too much and Judy returned to drugs. This time, Judy went straight to Louis B. and asked to be released from her contract. She didn't know if she could work anymore. "L.B." sympathized with Judy, but encouraged her to finish the movie and stay with MGM.

Judy went back to work, but her addiction affected her performance. It also made her grumpy and unpleasant to work with. The film lost money for MGM, though it did produce one of Judy's best-known songs, *Get Happy**, written by her old friend

Harold Arlen. None of this, however, made MGM or Judy happy.

L.B. gave Judy one more chance, but after a month of rehearsals for her new movie, he fired her from the film *Royal Wedding*. Three months later, he released her from her contract.

At first Judy was sad to leave MGM, but then she followed the advice in Harold's song and got happy. Judy saw this as the perfect opportunity to finally quit drugs and take her career in a new direction. The only problem was, she had no idea what direction to take.

Happier Times: Mickey Rooney, Judy Garland, and Louis B. Mayer enjoying milkshakes.

JUDY'S NAME IN LIGHTS

After leaving MGM, Judy discovered there was no Yellow Brick Road she could follow to keep her career going. That's when she remembered something else from *The Wizard of Oz*: "There's no place like home."

Judy was going back to where it all started—the stage.

Judy's new manager, Sid Luft, crafted a plan to rebuild her career. He scheduled several radio appearances so Judy could show the world she still had a wonderful voice. She even joked that the only reason she left MGM was because "Leo the Lion (the MGM mascot) bit me!" Next, Judy's mentor

A young Judy at the piano with Roger Edens

and friend, Roger Edens, helped her put together an act of old favorites like *Over the Rainbow* and *Get Happy*, plus new songs like *Rock-A-Bye Your Baby With a Dixie Melody***. In April, 1951, just seven months after MGM released her from her contract,

Judy performed at the London Palladium, one of the best concert halls in the world. She belted out tune after tune six nights a week, and when it was over, the theater manager exclaimed that he'd never heard such loud applause. Judy finally realized what she had been missing all these years: an audience. She was having almost as much fun as she had at the New Grand twenty-five years ago.

Judy at the London Palladium

Finally, after three months of touring England, Ireland, and Scotland, Judy headed to the one place her parents always dreamed of performing—Broadway. Of course, it was a risky move. Judy wasn't doing the same show she did in London. Instead, she was creating an old-style vaudeville act even though everyone said, "Vaudeville is dead." But Judy insisted, believing people would pay to see a family show. She added funny sketches and dance routines to her act, and looked like she was having fun. The show was an **immense** success, selling out every night for nineteen weeks. Five months later Judy won a special Tony Award for bringing back vaudeville.

Judy now took her show on the road, but for all her success, something was missing. Her personal life was still a mess, at least until she found love again, this time with the man who was busy keeping her a star. Judy married Sid Luft in the summer of 1952, and later that year gave birth to her second daughter, Lorna. Six-year-old Liza had a little sister!

By 1953, Judy was eager to get back into pictures, and Sid had the perfect project: a remake of a film called *A Star Is Born*. Judy had done a radio play of *A Star Is Born* in 1942 and thought it was a great idea. Sid asked George Cukor to direct. Cukor had turned down a chance to make the original movie, so he quickly agreed.

Filming began in October, 1953, but after two weeks, Sid and the bosses at Warner Bros. Studios thought the movie looked awful. They destroyed all the film and started over. Then the music director quit because he hated the way Judy performed the songs. Once again, Roger Edens came to the rescue and took over as music director, working with Judy to get the songs just right. After eight months, the movie about a young actress rising to fame was done, but Judy was nervous. She hadn't been in a movie in four years. Would it be a big success or had film audiences forgotten her?

The Hollywood premiere turned out to be bigger than the Academy Awards that year. Thousands of people lined the streets and millions more watched on TV as one movie star after the other arrived at the theater. Even George Jessel showed up to pay tribute to his old friend, joking about how he gave her the name Garland. Of course, he added, "Not that it would have made any difference. You couldn't hide that great talent if you'd called her Tel Aviv Windersill." Twenty years later and George was still kidding about her name!

The film was a critical success and awards poured

in. Judy won a Golden Globe for Best Actress and was nominated for an Oscar, but she had to skip the awards show. The day before the Oscars, Judy gave birth to her first son, Joey. TV cameras were set up in her hospital room so she could make her thank you speech if she won. And just about everybody expected her to win. When actor William Holden leaned into the microphone to announce the winner, the TV cameras stayed tight on Judy's face. Then Holden said, "The award for best actress goes to… Grace Kelly."

Judy couldn't believe it. She was sure she was going to win. Comedian Groucho Marx said Judy's loss was "the biggest robbery since Brinks (an armored car company)." Judy hid her devastation from the cameras and made the best of it by saying "Joey was the best Academy Award she could ever receive." Newspapers later reported that Judy lost by only six votes, but it was enough for Judy to stay away from Hollywood for a while. She stuck with stage and TV appearances where she felt more appreciated.

Color film had always been good to Judy, and the CBS television network decided to take a chance— they let Judy star in their first full-color TV show. The fact that most people only had black-and-white TV sets and couldn't see it in color didn't make a difference. The *Ford Star Jubilee* ended up being the highest-rated entertainment program for CBS that year and led Judy into a long relationship with the network. The following year, on November 3, 1956, CBS broadcast *The Wizard of Oz* on TV for the first time. Bert Lahr (also known as the Cowardly Lion) hosted the movie with ten-year-old Liza by his side. Three years later, CBS broadcast *The Wizard of Oz* again and turned it into a once-a-year holiday movie for decades to come.

The Most Watched Movie of All Time

Thanks to TV, T*he Wizard of Oz* is the most watched movie of all time. It's believed that more than one billion people have seen it!

Judy continued to appear on stage, television, and radio for the next few years, but none of those years were like 1961. At the age of thirty-nine, she was about to have one of the best years of her career. It began with an April show at New York City's legendary Carnegie Hall. Judy sang many of her best-known songs, bringing the audience to its feet until they stood at the foot of the stage just to be near her. Her powerful voice and emotional **timbre** captured every song perfectly. The audience cheered until Judy gave them several **encores,** and when she had no more songs to sing, they let her repeat some of her favorites. Critics have called Judy's performance "The greatest night in show business history." Later that year, Capitol Records released *Judy at Carnegie Hall* to rave reviews. The album shot up the charts and remained the number one record in the country for thirteen weeks. It won five Grammy Awards, including Album of the Year, the first time a woman won that award.

Judy also returned to acting in 1961—only it wasn't a musical. She appeared in *Judgment at Nuremberg*, a drama about the trial of Nazi war criminals after World War II. Some people worried the role was too serious for her, but Judy turned in a riveting

An Old Joke:

"How do you get to Carnegie Hall?"

"Practice, practice, practice!"

performance as a woman accused of illegally making friends with a Jewish man in Nazi Germany. She received her second Academy Award nomination, this time for Best Supporting Actress. Ironically, she lost to Rita Moreno for her work in *West Side Story*—a musical!

Although Judy continued to make movies, including the 1962 animated film *Gay Purr-ee* in which she played a cartoon cat in love with the city of Paris, she soon turned to television full-time. She taped another highly rated special for CBS. It was the second most-watched program of 1962 and earned four Emmy Award nominations, including one for Judy as the best performer in a variety show. CBS finally offered Judy her own series. The network wanted her on the air every week, not just once in a while. *The Judy Garland Show* debuted in September, 1963, after CBS met Judy's biggest demand: Mickey Rooney had to be her first guest because, she said, "He's my partner." Mickey and Judy sang a few playful songs in between jokes about their days making movies at MGM. It was clear that after thirty years, they were still best friends.

The first episode (which did not feature Mickey Rooney since CBS aired the episodes out of order) was a big success. It appeared CBS had a runaway hit on its hand after *The Judy Garland Show* scored higher ratings than *Bonanza*, the most popular show on TV. Many of Judy's movie and theater friends, including Ray Bolger and George Jessel, quickly signed up to be guest stars. Even her three children—Liza, Lorna, and Joey—sang and danced on the show, but trouble was brewing. Despite all the big-name talent and early interest, people at home stopped watching. The comedy sketches weren't very funny, and many of the jokes were insults about Judy's height, film failures, or other problems. Judy used all her talent to keep the show on the air, but the weekly grind of performing under the hot TV lights proved too much. In March, 1964, Judy told CBS she was canceling the show.

Although it appeared to be a ratings failure, *The Judy Garland Show* received four Emmy nominations, just like her 1962 special. And just like her special, it didn't win any. Once again, Judy was facing a career failure. Only this time, she didn't have Sid Luft to help her stay on top. Sid and Judy had separated two years earlier. She was on her own. Performing around the world and guest starring on television shows, all while raising a family, would test Judy's **stamina**—and she had to wonder if she could do it anymore.

THE SONG IS OVER

Just two months after Judy pulled the plug on her TV show, she was back on stage in Australia. The first two shows were terrific, but on the third night, Judy tried to perform while on medication. Although her voice still sounded good, she wandered around the stage as if lost and kept mumbling into the microphone. When the audience got angry with her, Judy argued back. She ended the concert early and walked out of the theater. The night was a disaster, but things were about to get worse.

Judy left Australia for Hong Kong, China, just days before a typhoon slammed into the city. She took several pills to help her sleep and stop her fear, but this time she didn't wake up. Her new boyfriend rushed her to the hospital where doctors stuck a tube down her throat and pumped her stomach to get the drugs out. Judy lapsed into a coma that lasted for more than half a day. Newspapers began reporting that the great Judy Garland was dead.

Doctors managed to save her life, but told Judy she shouldn't sing for at least a year. Judy, however, wasn't about to wait that long, and took the stage a few days later while still in Hong Kong. When she returned to America, she kept right on singing, both on stage and TV. She even returned to London to perform two shows with eighteen-year-old Liza at the Palladium. She recorded several more albums and continued to tour the United States and Europe. No matter what the doctors told her, Judy would not slow down.

In 1967, 20th Century-Fox gave Judy her last chance to star in a movie. One of the young characters was even based on Judy. At first, the studio was excited to hire her and met all of Judy's requests, including letting her have a pool table in her dressing room, but once filming started, she proved hard to work with. For the second time, a movie studio had to fire Judy Garland. However, they let her keep her costume from the film, a sparkly red outfit that looked like a pants suit copy of Dorothy's ruby slippers. Judy liked it so much that she ordered two more copies and wore them in concert. And over the next two years, there were a lot of concerts.

Judy performed repeatedly in New York City, plus Las Vegas, San Francisco, Philadelphia, Houston, Boston, Washington, D.C., and London. She gave her last concert in Copenhagen, the capital of Denmark, in March, 1969. She appeared sick, as if she would fall down, but her voice was strong, and critics praised her performance.

Judy in Copenhagen

Three months later, Judy was back in London. Her new husband, Mickey Deans, woke up on the morning of June 22 to find Judy missing. He banged on the locked bathroom door, but there was no answer. Desperate to find his wife, Mickey crawled out on the roof to look through the bathroom window. To his horror, he found Judy dead. Doctors said she died of an accidental drug overdose.

TV and radio stations immediately reported that the great Judy Garland, known to the world as the innocent and lovable Dorothy, had died. Her fans were shocked. More than 22,000 people passed through the funeral home to pay their last respects, and many placed flowers at her star on the Hollywood Walk of Fame. They struggled to cope with the loss of a legend, a singer whose sad but powerful voice reached them deep inside, but they had to accept that one of the greatest stars of Hollywood's Golden Age was gone. The woman Fred Astaire called "the greatest entertainer who ever lived" would entertain no more.

JUDY GARLAND'S LEGACY

Judy Garland's legacy begins with her children. Toward the end of Judy's life, Liza started getting movie offers. She asked her mother what she thought of a script called *The Sterile Cuckoo*. Judy liked it, and so Liza agreed to star in the film. Judy didn't live long enough to see it on screen, but her faith in her daughter's talent was rewarded. Not only was Liza nominated for an Oscar as Best Actress for *The Sterile Cuckoo*, she is one of the few performers to win every major award—an Oscar, Emmy, Grammy, and Tony. And although Joey Luft left show business as he got older, Lorna stayed with the family business and became a top Broadway star and singer.

Liza Minnelli   *Lorna Luft*

Beyond her children, however, Judy's impact on entertainment is huge. During the last eighteen years of her life, she made more than 1,000 concert appearances, plus hundreds more with her sisters from 1924-1935. She appeared on TV and radio more than 300 times, and her films are still shown around the world, none more than *The Wizard of Oz*. Hundreds of millions of people have grown up with Judy Garland in their lives.

Although she won a Juvenile Academy Award in 1940, a Tony Award in 1952, and a Grammy in 1962, Judy received dozens of other awards and nominations, including three Emmy nominations. She had fifteen hit records, and the American Film Institute (AFI) lists five of her songs among the top 100 movie songs of all time. Of course, *Over the*

Rainbow is at the top, and is in the Grammy Hall of Fame, along with *Judy at Carnegie Hall*, *(Dear Mr. Gable) You Made Me Love You*, and several other tunes.

Judy Garland's Top Movie Songs

1. *Over the Rainbow (The Wizard of Oz)*

11. *The Man That Got Away (A Star Is Born)*

26. *The Trolley Song (Meet Me in St. Louis)*

61. *Get Happy (Summer Stock)*

76. *Have Yourself a Merry Little Christmas (Meet Me in St. Louis)*

The AFI also ranks Judy as the eighth greatest female star in movie history, so it's quite fitting that she have two stars on the Hollywood Walk of Fame—one for acting and one for singing. She even has imprints of her hands and feet in concrete. If you're ever in Los Angeles and want to see just how tiny Judy Garland really was, visit Grauman's Chinese Theater and see how you measure up!

Judy puts her hand in concrete outside
Grauman's Chinese Theatre

Judy received plenty of awards outside Hollywood, too. She has appeared on two U.S. postage stamps, and her hometown of Grand Rapids, Minnesota, has a Judy Garland Museum, with the perfect motto: "There's No Place Like Home!" There have been more than a dozen books about her, as well as several TV specials. Lorna's own book about her mother, *Me and My Shadows: A Family Memoir*, was turned into a movie.

Many of the books about Judy talk about the dark side of her life because part of her legacy is her drug addiction. Judy's life is an example of overcoming so many problems on your way to success—of not taking "No" for an answer when it seems everyone is turning you down—but it is also a warning not to let drugs take away your talent and your dreams.

Judy Garland was one of the brightest stars of Hollywood's Golden Age. She was a natural entertainer who loved being in front of an audience and may have been, as Mickey Rooney said, "the greatest talent to ever trod the boards." She could dance, act, tell jokes, and most of all, sing. Judy could fill a theater with her voice and touch people in the back row. She may have only been 4'11", but Judy Garland was a BIG talent, and people will enjoy her movies and her music for decades to come.

Judy Garland's grave, where fans still leave
mementos decades after her death

TIMELINE

1913	Frank Gumm meets Ethel Milne.
1914-1917	World War I fought.
1915	Mary Jane Gumm born.
1917	Dorothy Virginia Gumm born.
1922	Frances Ethel Gumm born.
1924	"Baby" Gumm takes the stage for the first time.

1926	The Gumms move to California.
June 1929	The Gumm Sisters appear in their first movie.
October 1929	The Great Depression begins.
1934	Frances Gumm becomes Judy Garland.
1936	Judy signs with MGM.
1937	Judy has her first hit records.
August 1939	*The Wizard of Oz* released.
1939-1945	World War II fought. The United States enters the war in 1941.
1940	Judy wins a Juvenile Academy Award.
1944	*Meet Me in St. Louis* released.

1945-1946	The Nuremberg Trials held.
1946	Liza Minnelli born.
1950	Judy Garland let go by MGM.
1950-1953	The Korean War fought.
1952	Lorna Luft born.
1953	Judy's mother dies.
1954	*A Star Is Born* released.
1955	Joey Luft born.
1956	*The Wizard of Oz* airs on TV for the first time.
July 1961	*Judy at Carnegie Hall* released.
December 1961	*Judgment at Nuremberg* released.
1962-1973	U.S. involved in the Vietnam War.

March 1963	Martin Luther King, Jr. leads the March on Washington.
November 1963	President John F. Kennedy shot.
1963-1964	*The Judy Garland Show* airs.
June 1969	Judy Garland dies in England.
July 1969	Neil Armstrong walks on the moon.
1973	Liza Minnelli wins an Oscar for *Cabaret*.
1975	The Judy Garland Museum opens.
1981	*Over the Rainbow* inducted into the Grammy Hall of Fame.
1989	Judy Garland pictured on a U.S. postage stamp.
2006	Judy Garland pictured on another U.S. postage stamp.

HISTORICAL FIGURES

Fred Astaire (1899-1987): Considered one of the greatest dancers of Hollywood's Golden Age, he is best known for his movies with fellow dancer Ginger Rogers.

L. Frank Baum (1856-1919): A prolific writer of fantasy novels and short stories, L. Frank Baum wrote *The Wonderful Wizard of Oz* and its thirteen sequels.

 **Charlie Chaplin (1889-1977):** The greatest comedian of the Silent Film Era made his Little Tramp one of the best known faces in movie history.

George Cukor (1899-1983): One of the first directors to work in "talkies," Cukor directed several now classic films including *The Philadelphia Story, Gaslight,* and *My Fair Lady.* He played a major role in shaping the look of *The Wizard of Oz.*

Deanna Durbin (1921-2013): Judy Garland's chief rival for parts in her early days at MGM, Durbin won the Juvenile Academy Award in 1938.

Victor Fleming (1889-1949): A World War I photographer, Fleming later directed both silent films and talkies, including *The Wizard of Oz* and *Gone With the Wind.* He is the only director to have two films inside the top ten best movies ever made.

 **Clark Gable (1901-1960):** Known as The King of Hollywood, Gable worked as an extra in silent films before breaking through in talkies. His most famous role was Rhett Butler in *Gone With the Wind.*

George Jessel (1898-1981): "Georgie" Jessel was a comedian, actor, and movie producer who gave The Garland Sisters their name.

Lorna Luft (born 1952): Judy Garland's second child is a singer and actress known for her work in movies, TV, and Broadway.

Sid Luft (1915-2005): Judy Garland's third husband was a film producer who helped get her career back on track after she was released by MGM.

Louis B. Mayer (1884-1957): Known as Louis B. or L.B., Mayer built MGM into the biggest studio in Hollywood and the most successful of Hollywood's Golden Age.

Ethel Meglin (1890-1988): A former dancer in movies, Meglin founded one of the top dance studios in Hollywood, training Judy Garland, Shirley Temple, Mickey Rooney and many other child stars.

Liza Minnelli (born 1946): Judy Garland's oldest child is an actress and singer in movies, TV, and Broadway. Liza is one of only a few entertainers to win Emmy, Grammy, Oscar, and Tony awards.

Vincente Minnelli (1903-1986): Judy Garland's second husband directed several classic movies, including the Judy Garland musical *Meet Me in St. Louis.* He is the father of Liza Minnelli.

Mickey Rooney (1920-2014): Mickey Rooney began his career as a baby in his parents' Broadway show and appeared in his first movie at age six. He was good at both comedy and drama, and won an Oscar and Emmy for his acting. He appeared in more than 300 movies and TV shows, from silent films to talkies, including *National Velvet, The Black Stallion, Santa Claus Is Coming to Town,* and *Night at the Museum.* It's even said Mickey Mouse is named after him!

Mack Sennett (1880-1960): An Academy Award-winning director known as The King of Comedy, Mack Sennett discovered and directed some of the best-known silent film comedians, including Charlie Chaplin, Harold Lloyd, and The Keystone Cops.

Shirley Temple (1928-2014): Probably the biggest child star ever, she appeared in her first movie at age three and became a star at four. From 1935-1938, she was the number one box office star. As an adult, she went into politics and became a diplomat, representing the United States in foreign countries.

John Wayne (1907-1979): Born Marion Morrison, John Wayne is the most famous movie cowboy of them all. He was an All-American football player at the University of Southern California before becoming an actor. He won an Oscar for the 1952 film *The Quiet Man*.

Florenz Ziegfeld (1869-1932): A Broadway producer who created musicals for the stage and movies. He was married to Billie Burke, who played Glinda the Good Witch in *The Wizard of Oz*!

GLOSSARY

Château: A large or fancy French country house

Encore: an additional performance after the regular concert is over, typically given if an audience asks for it by loud applause or cheering.

Honorary: A title or award given out of respect rather than being earned.

Immense: huge.

Matinee: an afternoon show.

Mesmerize: to captivate or hold someone's attention as if he or she is in a spell.

Morale: the feelings a person or group has about a task or duty.

Rendition: a particular version of a song.

Revenue: Money or income.

Sentimental: Showing sadness.

Stamina: strength or energy.

Timbre: the sound quality of a voice or musical instrument.

PHOTOGRAPHS

Page 8: **Josephine Baker dancing the Charleston at the Foiles-Bergères, Paris** by French Walery, 1926

Page 9: **Judy Garland birth house with snow in Grand Rapids, Minnesota** by Matt Anderson, 2005

Page 13: **Publicity photo for John Wayne in** *The Comancheros* from 20th Century-Fox, 1961

Page 19: **Dwellers in Circleville's "Hooverville," Central Ohio** by Ben Shahn, Summer, 1938, *Library of Congress Prints and Photographs*

Page 21: Publicity photo from *Love Finds Andy Hardy* by Clarence Bull/MGM, 1938

Page 24: Publicity photo from *Bright Eyes,* Fox Film Corp./20th Century-Fox, 1934

Page 29: Judy Garland performing *Bill* **at the Chicago World's Fair,** July, 1934

Page 36: Publicity photo of Judy Garland's first day at MGM, October 1, 1935

Page 45: Screenshot from *Love Finds Andy Hardy,* directed by George B. Seitz, MGM, 1938

Page 48: Girl in an iron lung, Children's Hospital, Boston, Massachusetts

Page 57: Lana Turner, screenshot from *The Postman Always Rings Twice,* directed by Tay Garnett, MGM, 1946

Page 58: Judy Garland and Mickey Rooney with soldiers at the Hollywood Canteen, Hollywood, California

Page 63: Mickey Rooney, Judy Garland, and Louis B. Mayer have milkshakes, MGM publicity photo, 1939

Page 65: Judy Garland and Roger Eden at the piano, circa 1938

Page 66: Judy Garland at the London Palladium by Cornell Capa, 1951

Page 72: Carnegie Hall, New York (Skewed) by David Samuel, 2010

Page 77: Judy Garland in concert at the Falkoner Center, March 25, 1969

Page 80: Liza Minnelli as Sally Bowles in the film *Cabaret* from Allied Artists Picture Corporation, January 19, 1972

Page 80: Singer Lorna Luft by Phil Konstantin, May 20, 2007

Page 82: Mickey Rooney watching Judy Garland put handprint in cement at Grauman's Theatre during "Babes in Arms" film premiere, **1939,** Los Angeles Times/UCLA Library, October 25, 1939

Page 84: Judy Garland's crypt at the Ferncliff Mausoleum by Judyfan1922, August 22, 2007

Page 89: Publicity photo for Fred Astaire in *You'll Never Get Rich*, Columbia Pictures, 1941

Page 90: Screenshot of Charlie Chaplin in *The Kid* directed by Charles Chaplin, Charles Chaplin Productions, 1921

Page 91: Publicity photo for Clark Gable in *Gone With the Wind,* MGM, 1939

Page 92: Mack Sennett in an advertisement for **Moving World Pictures** by Fred Hartsook, July 1916

Page 93: Florenz Ziegfeld, circa 1920

And see plenty of Judy Garland videos at *johnbriggsbooks.net!*

REFERENCE MATERIALS

Books

Clarke, Gerald. *Get Happy: The Life of Judy Garland,* Delta, 2001

Scott Schneider. *Judy Garland: The Day-by-Day Chronicles of a Legend,* Taylor Trade Publishing, 2006

Websites

Biography.com, *Judy Garland*

Internet Movie Database, *Judy Garland and related links to film*

JudyGarland.com

Judy Garland Database

The Judy Room, *Timeline*

Oz.Wikia, *Betty Danko*

Sherwood Times Great Entertainers, *The Gumm Sisters*

Wikipedia, *Judy Garland*

Television

A Star Is Born World Premiere. September 29, 1954. NBC

Private Screenings. Robert Osborne interviews Mickey Rooney, April 1, 1997, Turner Classic Movies

The Mike Douglas Show. Mike Douglas interviews Judy Garland, August 16, 1968, Syndicated

The Today Show. Barbara Walters interviews Judy Garland, March 6, 1967, NBC

ALSO FROM

ATOMBANK'S

BIG BIOGRAPHY SERIES

MARY DYER, FRIEND OF FREEDOM

UPCOMING BOOKS

PETE SEEGER, THE PEOPLE'S SINGER

JIM THORPE, ATHLETE OF THE CENTURY

LOOK FOR THEM AT

ATOMBANKBOOKS.COM!